12 Divertimentos for Solo Mandolin by James Oswald

Arranged and Adapted by John Goodin

WWW.MELBAY.COM

About the Author

John Goodin (1951-) is from southern Indiana and began playing the guitar shortly after seeing the Beatles on the Ed Sullivan show in February of 1964. Ten years later he began to play the mandolin. He has played in many bands and ensembles performing music in a variety of styles and was a founding member of the Louisville Mandolin Orchestra in 1988. Along with studying folk, jazz and pop music he has attended workshops offered by several of today's finest classical mandolinists and he is a long time member of the Classical Mandolin Society of America.

As a composer Goodin has written many pieces for mandolin orchestra that have been recorded and performed by mandolin orchestras in Europe, Australia, Japan and the United States. Joachim-Trekel-Musikverlag has published three of his mandolin orchestra pieces, *The Louisville Suite* (1995), *Heavens On Earth* (2006) and *Antonina* (2015). His contra dance band, Contratopia, has recorded over 40 of his tunes on their four CDs: *Hands Four, Ballroom Echoes, Smitten* and *Riff City*. Additionally, he has released a duo CD with fiddler Erik Sessions, *Notes from the Farm* (2012), and two solo CDs, *Mandolin Tunes* (2011) and *Deer Tracks for Solo Mandolin* (2013).

Mel Bay Publications published Goodin's book *Telemann for Mandolin* in 2010 and he has self-published the *Contratopia Tunebook* (with Erik Sessions, 2001), *31 Waltzes* (2009) and *Midwestern Mandolin Duos* (2010). His music has also appeared in Don Julin's *Mandolin For Dummies*, August Watters' book *Exploring Classical Mandolin* and volume 3 of the *Portland Collection*. Goodin has lived in Decorah, Iowa since 1994 where he is now an Emeritus professor affiliated with Luther College.

Introduction

James Oswald (1710-1769) was a Scottish composer, music teacher and publisher who moved to London and was quite active there from 1741 until the early 1760s. Around 1759 he composed and published a set of twelve pieces (*Twelve Divertimentis for the Guittar, Dedicated to Her Grace the Dutchess of Grafton*) for the popular wire-strung "guittar", a type of cittern that had become fashionable in society.

Oswald's original music is all in the key of C major. The "guittar" in question, often labeled the English guitar today, had six courses of wire strings and was most commonly tuned c,e,g,c',e',g'. All twelve divertimentos could be played in the instrument's first position and Oswald took advantage of the instrument's tuning to include numerous passages in thirds.

In adapting this fine music for the modern mandolin I first transposed the pieces into different keys, partly for variety and partly to follow Oswald's intention of keeping the music mostly in the first position. I also simplified many of the double-stop passages to make them more mandolin-friendly. I have retained Oswald's interesting orthography and I have transcribed his few dynamic markings, although I have used *p* and *f* where he commonly used *Dolce* and *For.*

In 2001 Rob MacKillop produced a recording of the original *Divertimentis* played on an authentic 18th century guittar which I highly recommend both for pleasure and for guidance in matters of performance practice. These short and friendly divertimentos have given me much pleasure over the last few years and I hope that you will enjoy them also.

Contents

Divertimento I 5

Divertimento II 9

Divertimento III 13

Divertimento IV 16

Divertimento V 20

Divertimento VI 24

Divertimento VII 28

Divertimento VIII 31

Divertimento IX 34

Divertimento X 37

Divertimento XI 41

Divertimento XII 44

Divertimento I

James Oswald, arr. Goodin

Amoroso

Vivace alon Presto

Gavota Moderato

Divertimento II

James Oswald, arr. Goodin

Affetuoso Moderato

Tempo di Minuett

Gavotto Moderato

Divertimento III

James Oswald, arr. Goodin

Amoroso Largo

Allegro Moderato

Andante

Divertimento IV

James Oswald, arr. Goodin

Affetuoso Largo

Gavotta Moderato

Aria Andante

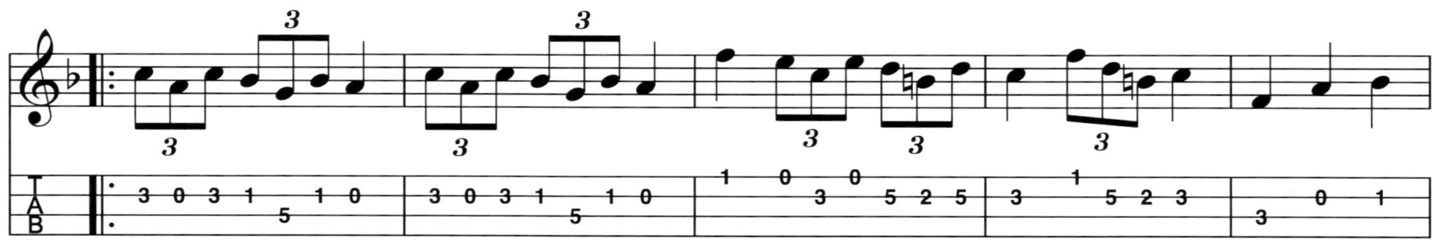

Con Spirito Moderato

T
A
B

Divertimento V

James Oswald, arr. Goodin

Allegro Moderato

Pastorale Andante

Tempo di Minuetto

Divertimento VI

James Oswald, arr. Goodin

Amoroso Largo

Moderato Lento

Pastorali Vivace

Affetuoso Andante

This page has been left blank to avoid awkward page turns.

Divertimento VII

James Oswald, arr. Goodin

Affetuoso Largo

Adagio

Tempo di Minuetto

Divertimento VIII

James Oswald, arr. Goodin

Andante Affeta

Vivace
p
f
p
f
p
f
p
f
p
f

Tempo di Minuetto

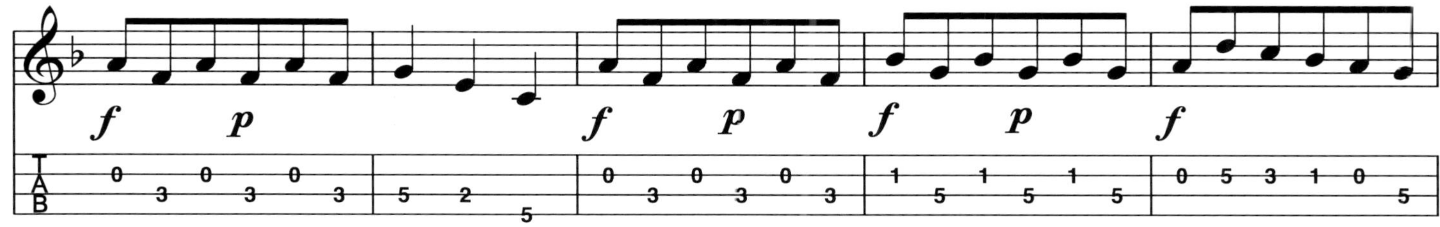

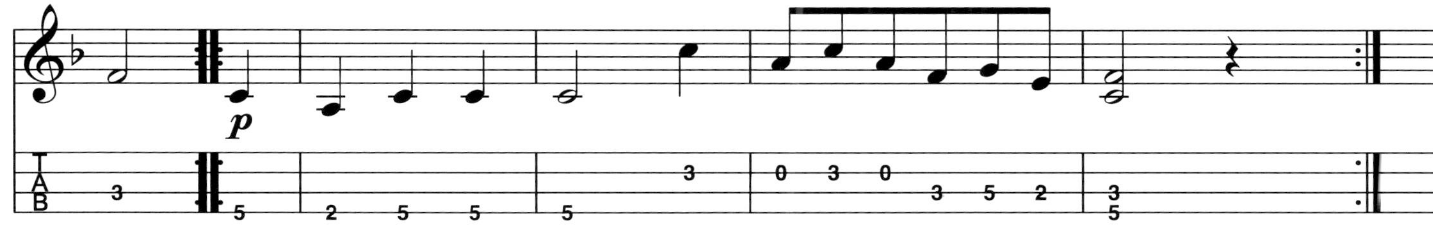

Divertimento IX

James Oswald, arr. Goodin

Gratioso Largo

Mussetto Moderato

Andante con Spirito

Divertimento X

James Oswald, arr. Goodin

Amoroso Larghetto

Allegro Moderato

Andante

Adagio

Giga Andante

Divertimento XI

James Oswald, arr. Goodin

Allegro Moderato

Cantable Andante

p
f
p

Divertimento XII

James Oswald, arr. Goodin

Largo

p

Moderato con Spirio

TAB
p
f

p
p
f
Amoroso
p
f

Giga Vivace

WWW.MELBAY.COM